POEMS FROM THE HEART

ERNEST R. WALLACE

POEMS FROM THE HEART
Copyright © 2014 by Ernest R. Wallace

ISBN: 978-09831072-31
Library of Congress Control Number: 2016954848

All rights reserved
No part of this book may be reproduced or transmitted in any form or by any means electronic or mechanical, including photocopying, recording, or by any information storage and retrieval system, without permission in writing from the author, except for the use of brief quotations in a book review.

Printed in the United States of America

Published by: Jazzi Creations Publishing Service

Cover Design Book Layout by:
Jazzi Creations Publishing Service
Chicago, Illinois
Website: www.jazzicreations.com

Senior Editor: J. D. Cooper
Copy Editor: Talia Lambarki
Proofreader: Judy A. Wallace

Poems From The Heart

1 Corinthians 12:28-31

28 And God hath set some in the church, first apostles, secondarily prophets, thirdly teachers, after that miracles, then gifts of healings, helps, governments, diversities of tongues.

29 Are all apostles? Are all prophets? Are all teachers? Are all workers of miracles?

30 Have all the gifts of healing? Do all speak with tongues? Do all interpret?

31 But covet earnestly the best gifts: and yet shew I unto you a more excellent way.

1 Corinthians 13:1-3

1 Though I speak with the tongues of men and of angels, and have not charity, I am become as sounding brass, or a tinkling cymbal.

2 And though I have the gift of prophecy, and understand all mysteries, and all knowledge; and though I have all faith, so that I could remove mountains, and have not charity, I am nothing.

3 And though I bestow all my goods to feed the poor, and though I give my body to be burned, and have not charity, it profiteth me nothing. *King James Version of the Bible.

Dedication

Theses poems were written as a memoriam to my mother Mrs. Parthenia Wallace.

TABLE OF CONTENTS
SECTION I: THEOLOGICAL POEMS

Reverend Williams And Reverent Wisdom	2
Like Father Like Son	3
What Did Jesus Write In The Sand?	4
The Queen Mother	5
Greater Bethlehem's President Washington	6
Prayers From The Other Side Of The Ceiling	7
Our Busy God	8
No Room In The Inn	9
My Lord, My Shepherd	10
Jesus And Julia	11
The Holy Spirit	12
Hallelujah Anyhow	13
Granny	14
Good Morning God	15
First Lady	16
Memorial To Edna Mae Barnett	17
Divine Love	18
A Dialogue With Jesus	20
A Credo To God	21
Chairman Of The Board	22
Our Evangelist...Charlene Johnson	23
A Poem Dedicated To Mrs. Cecelia Bozeman	24
Who Was Adam's Mother?	25
Beyond The Reach Of God	26
The Second Creation	28
Angels Then And Now	29
No Prayer, No Power, No Love	30

SECTION II: SOCIOLOGICAL POEMS

When Roses Last In The Dooryard Bloomed	32
When You Fail	33
What I Don't Know	34
Weak As Chinese Tea	35
Ode To The Pharaoh With No Nose	36
A Letter To Socrates	37
The Negro Question	38
I Cannot Change My Name To Pawlikowski	40
Love...American Style	42
God Is Not A Republican	43
An Ode To Gwendolyn Brooks	44
The Flight Of A Dream	45
Eaama, Eaama, To Thee I Sing!	46
A Country That Loses Its Love	47
Real American Freedom	48
A Man Called King	50
America: Black And White	52

SECTION III: POEMS OF SECULAR LOVE

Yours..Now, Henceforth And Forevermore	54
The Special Touch	56
Parthenia's Children	57
Ode To A Lost Love	58
I Dream Of Nancy	59
Our Majestic Royal Love	60
The Magic Of Autumn	61
The Love Of My Life	62
I Must Go Down To The Sea	63
A Grecian Musical Ode	64
Five Minutes To Two	65
The First Spring Thaw	66
The Baby No One Can Hold	67
As I Lay Dying	68
To Have Lost At Love Three Times	69
My Brother Arther W. Wallace	70
Author's Profile	

SECTION I
THEOLOGICAL POEMS

REVEREND WILLIAMS AND REVERENT WISDOM

Williams and wisdom go hand in hand
Our pastor knows "The Master's Plan"
He understands the Word of God
We can't stop now where the saints have trod
Abraham had faith, Moses had a staff
The Apostles preached and left us a path
When...**you find the old way walk therein**
Constrain men to Christ and away from sin
The Patriarchs did their job in their day
We must Take up our cross and now show the way
Our pastor tells us we need peace from within
Before we can try to be any man's friend
You can't love anyone if you don't love yourself
Put jealousy and pride back on the shelf
Pastor Williams tells us we have two things to do
Bring yourself to Christ
and your brother with you!!!

A Poem Dedicated To My Pastor,
The Rev. Dr. I. W. Williams Sr.

Like Father, Like Son

Reverend Robert is our pastor's son
He's carrying on the work that his father has begun
He teaches and preaches and shows us the way
He's a great example in our church today
He strikes a match and starts a burn
He then lets us know when it's our turn
We must hold up the "Banner"
and take up our "cross"
"And let our lights shine" to a world that is lost
We must follow our preachers as they follow the Lord
And all march to Zion to claim our reward
Our Lord is coming as he said he would
To Rapture the saved and not just the good
The first time he came in humility
He walked on the waters and calmed the sea
His first miracle turned water into wine
He spat on the ground and gave sight to the blind
He's coming again in power and might
He's coming again, "As a thief in the night."
Preachers keep preaching and choirs sing your songs
His reward will be with him and it won't be long.

What Did Jesus Write in the Sand?

What did Jesus write in the sand?
What he wrote we wouldn't understand
He made some scratches
He made some marks
What he wrote he could have written in the dark
What he described no man could discern
What he did was for all to learn
Be careful when you point and accuse
What applies to others applies to you
The woman's critics brought her to The Lord
When they looked up they got their reward
"If your Conscience Can't Condemn You
Neither Can I"
When the woman looked up no one…
no one was standing by…

The Queen Mother

Was she a queen first?
Or a mother first?
Or both at the same time
If she was in the rural south of the U.S.A
She would have a name of a different kind
She would be Big Mamma or Mother Dear
But loved just as well
Providence had her born in the U.K
So on her the mantle of royalty fell
Loving, gracious and kind to all
God granted her one hundred years
She died the day before Easter morn
And left the world in tears.

GREATER BETHLEHEM'S PRESIDENT WASHINGTON

George Washington, Harold Washington,
and Alice Washington
All leaders in their own right
Each carrying the torch of faith
and spreading God's glorious light
George was a general
Harold had generalship,
and Alice Washington
gives the bible class general leadership
George helped found a nation
Harold made Chicago great
The bible class under Alice Washington
as good as any in the state
Alice Washington and Rev. Robert
make a great teaching team
They teach the word and make us search
for what it really means
As gold is put in the furnace
and left there until it's pure
They teach us to search for God himself
so we can make our
salvation sure.

Prayers From the Other Side of the Ceiling

Sometimes when we pray
we're only talking to the ceiling
If we don't pray from the heart with faith
the prayer has no feeling
When we pray from the heart
with sincerity and truth
Our prayer gets to the other side of the ceiling
and goes beyond the roof
That from the heart reaches the heart
and God sends down some proof
That prayer is always answered
when done in spirit and truth
When you find yourself praying
and hear a ricochet
It only reached the ceiling
and bounded another way
Get back down on your knees
and pray like He's your friend
Pray with honesty and truth
then watch…new life…begin
Prayers from the other side of the ceiling.

OUR BUSY GOD

God sits on His throne
way out in the universe
Yes, He has a lot to do
but never too busy for earth
He makes sure the stars are in orbit
He makes the sun come up every day
Yes, He has a lot to do
but never to busy to hear us pray
How much time does it take
to keep the heavens in its place
and have enough ear to hear the human race?
He sits high and He looks low,
makes waves on the seas,
and makes the winds to blow
Sometimes we feel that He's not there
but when we pray
You know He still cares
His ways are not our ways
but He's been here for the length of days
when we reach our earthly ends
we will find that there is where

His real love begins.

No Room in the Inn

No room in the Inn
No room in the Inn
Baby Jesus was put out
So God would take us in
No room in the Inn
No room in the Inn
He was already on the road
To redeem our sins
His father is everywhere at the same time
The Virgin Mary for her baby
no place she could find
No place for "The King of Kings" to be born
But Herod in his palace was sad and forlorn
King Herod had shelter
and warm rooms in which to stay
"The Lord of Lords" had a barn
and was born on some hay
King Herod worried about
who would take his place
So he searched for the babe
sent to save the human race
Searched he did and he searched high and low
But the place of the newborn king
was only for wise men to know.

My Lord, My Shepherd

Who is this Lord my Shepherd?
That promises me eternal life
Who is this Lord, my Shepherd?
That watches me day and night
Who is this Lord, my Shepherd?
Who is this Lord, my Shepherd?
That calms my darkest fears
Who is this Lord, my Shepherd?
That wipes away all my tears
Who is this Lord My Shepherd
That says He's always near
Who is this Lord, my Shepherd
That makes my dark paths clear?
He's the alpha and Omega, in life, my best friend
He promised to be with me all the way to the end
When I'm lost and burdened,
He said He would be there
To comfort me and cheer me
and let me know He cares
When I feel I cannot make it and think I cannot stand
He sends His Holy Spirit and then gives me His hand
When I'm in the dark valley and have no place to go
He sends His peace and strength just to let me know
No weapon formed against you can last or endure
Your Shepherd can protect you,
of that you can be sure!

JESUS AND JULIA

My son David lives in Holly Springs, Mississippi
and their state tree is the Magnolia.
My mother was born down the road
in Memphis Tennessee
and her only daughter was named Julia
God had only one begotten son
Parthenia had only one daughter
One can be a lonely number,
but special and in divine order
Why some have only one son or daughter
only God can know
How the one through the passing of time
becomes more special is only for God to show
God's son had thirty and three years
Julia had sixty and nine
God promised we can have three score and ten
So, Julia left us just about on time.

The Holy Spirit

There is a force in the universe,
it's greater than you and you can use it
There is a force in the universe,
it's greater than you, and you must choose it
It is a light in darkness
and gives direction to your life
If you do not use its power
you will only end up in strife
It's older than man, the world and time
It was here before God made the sun,
stars, light and told them to shine
It was here when darkness
was upon the face of the deep
It was here when man needed a companion
and God put him to sleep
It was here before the first wind blew
It was here before the rain
and on the ground there was only dew
It was here before there was a when or a where
It is here today and can be found…everywhere
It started out in heaven and is now on earth
It cannot be bought but is free…with new birth,
The Holy Spirit!!!

Poems from the heart

HALLELUJAH ANYHOW

When things are going great – Hallelujah anyhow
When things are going bad – Hallelujah anyhow
When I'm reaching my goals – Hallelujah anyhow
When I'm failing my goals – Hallelujah anyhow
When I feel good – Hallelujah anyhow
When I feel bad – Hallelujah anyhow
When I feel wonderful – Hallelujah anyhow
When I feel rotten – Hallelujah anyhow
When people love me – Hallelujah anyhow
When people hate me – Hallelujah anyhow
When I'm understood – Hallelujah anyhow
When I'm misunderstood – Hallelujah anyhow
When I feel the power of God
Hallelujah anyhow
When I don't feel the presence of God at all
Hallelujah anyhow
When my mother and father understand
Hallelujah anyhow
When my mother and father put me out
Hallelujah anyhow
When I am strong and everything is working
Hallelujah anyhow
When I can't see my way out – Hallelujah anyhow
Hallelujah – when I'm up
Hallelujah – when I'm down
Hallelujah – when I feel there is no one around
Hallelujah, Hallelujah – Hallelujah anyhow!

GRANNY

Who is this lady called, "Granny?"
To me she is just an angel
Is she granny or Fanny… She's Fanny Bentley!
To me she is just an angel
When I have a problem, her words come to me
She's just like a guardian angel you see…
She says, "While you are trying to figure it out,
stop worrying about it
God has already worked it out."
To me she is just an angel
Some Sundays, I rise all tired and worn
And I remember Fannie Bentley said,
"Toot your own horn."
I stop wondering and worrying
and get out of the house
And rush on to church,
it's my father's business I'm about
Thank you Granny for being who you are
For in Greater Bethlehem
I don't have to wish upon a star
Stars are signs of angels here and there
When Granny is at church our angel is here!

GOOD MORNING GOD

How are you today?
I know you're very busy
But I just stopped to say
In relative time I feel old
But in real time I just got here
Another hour, another day,
another month and year
Whatever happens tomorrow
I just want You to be near
Our world is looking shaky again
Mankind is losing out,
but in Your Word You say
Be strong, have faith
and You will bring us out.
You're always in control
The world is in Your hands
You're not concerned about the schemes
of man, or any of his plans
You know what tomorrow holds
The future You've already seen
You created life, You created man,
You created everything
Thank You for being God all by Yourself
For You know what everything means
Thank You for today, for love and peace of mind
Thank You for waking me up all in my right mind.

First Lady

First is a special word and brings a lot of joy
Remember at Christmas time when you got your first toy
You received it with gladness and a lot of bliss
You knew nothing in the world could be better than this
An Olympic runner who comes in first he receives the gold
An NBA champion team
the trophy they get to hold
They hold it proudly and hold it high
In the locker room is the second place team
and you can hear them cry
The first is always better,
but second you can't demean
First carries with it honor and very high esteem
First gets the blue and gold
The story of second is very seldom told
Zelma Williams of first Greater Bethlehem
brings honor to our church
She is a special lady and she is our "First"
There's none that can come after her
and there's none who came before
She is our SPECIAL FIRST LADY
need I say anymore!

MEMORIAL TO EDNA MAE BARNETT

Life goes on and yet it won't be the same
without Edna Mae Barnett
The sweetest lady you could ever know
When you see her you'd just wave and say 10-4
We were her family and sometimes all she had
But when you saw her smile
she made you feel glad
Now she is resting in the arms of the Lord
Waiting for His return and her reward
She is gone before us to show us the way
The path we must travel some day
Paul said our citizenship is not here on earth
Luke said we got a ticket with our new birth
The trains in the station, but who's on board
No one knows, but Jesus our Lord.

DIVINE LOVE

Divine love comes all the way from God's throne
Divine love comes from God's house
and settles into your home
Divine love travels millions of miles
just to wrap around your heart
Divine love is just what it is
because it comes from God
You can't buy it, you can't steal it,
and Divine love is always free
It travels over mountains, over vast oceans
and rides upon the sea
It's the greatest thing you'll possess in life,
it makes it what it should be
It has no heights, it has no depths,
it has not east or west
It's the greatest thing life offers for you,
see it is God's best
It has no bottom, it has no top
and really has no end
You never know you have it
until you feel it from within
Oh, how wonderful, oh how great

It dominates the soul…
It never weakens, it never wears out
And it never really gets old
It's with you when you are awake
It's with you when you sleep
It makes you laugh and it makes you sing
And at times it makes you weak
Divine love is divine
Because it comes from God, you can't describe it, you can't explain it
But you know it's in your heart
Oh, what joy… oh what peace…
It's with you every day
It really never attains its best
Until you give it away…
Bow on your knees and look to God above
Start the day and fall in love
Then tell someone I love you
And watch what it does… for two.

A Dialogue with Jesus

Good Morning Lord
How are you today?
What's Up?
Don't forget about me okay, hook me up
I love you
People keep trying to use
all this psychology on me
You know—stimuli and response stuff
Running interference patterns on me
Talking about exploration and revolution
What! You say? "Don't worry about revolution,
worry about revelation."
That's right, You did talk to John on that island
called Patmos and he said that You'll be right back
Yes, Lord he said that You'll be right back
But that You will have something in Your hands
What did he say You will have
Oh! I think he said something like, this...
You will have justice in one hand
and reward in the other.

A Credo to God

Almighty God, most Powerful One,
in me Thy work has just begun
A dying world, a violent earth,
a cause, a need for peace: Rebirth.
Kill my brother! Kill my son!
Kill a priest! Kill anyone!
What happened to the world you've made?
To violence we've become a slave.
We search the planets, moon, and stars,
on earth we live our life in bars.
What can we do to help this race?
To make this world a better place.
To thee we pray for Divine insight,
what can we do to help our plight?
In a world of constant change,
You, alone, remain the same.
God, show us how to save our home,
before we come to Thy great throne.

This poem was published in the International Library of Poetry.

CHAIRMAN OF THE BOARD

How do you spell Deacon?
You spell it MURIL EMERSON
He's been with the Sunday school from day one
He loves his Sunday school
He loves his class
Every Sunday he's up to the task
When he reviews the lesson
You know a show down is due
Through tears and laughter
he brings the Word to you
I've been In his church over twenty-two years
When I come to Sunday school
I know Deacon Emerson is here
He use to say, "Look out class number one."
But not anymore…
because they're rough riders one by one
So Deacon stayed with class number eight
Where he remains a watchman at the gate.

Poems from the heart

OUR EVANGELIST…CHARLENE JOHNSON

Greater Bethlehem has a Pastor
and a Pastor Emeritus
Both called by God and a blessing to us
God blessed our church and sent another prize
He anointed Charlene Johnson to evangelize
She'll bring you God's Word
and won't bite her tongue
She's growing in grace
and climbing Jacobs Ladder rung by rung
Much is required of her
because much she has received
She's singing God's songs
and she's bringing in the sheaves,
God blessed her to bring us the Word,
She sings Zion's songs like none you have heard
We've had Sallie Martin and Mahalia Jackson too,
Thank God Greater Bethlehem
that God was not through
He sent us an evangelist and musician all in one
Charlene Johnson keep working for the Lord
until He says well done.

This poem is dedicated to Evangelist Charlene Johnson
of First Greater Bethlehem.

A Poem Dedicated to Mrs. Cecelia Bozeman

Cecelia Bozeman, Greater Bethlehem's flower
Cecelia Bozeman lady of the hour
To this church God had given us you
Three score, four score, five score and two
You were given to this church alone
A blessed, precious gift from God's own throne
The Lord has shown us His great grace
To have you worship in this place
We feel special we feel blessed
You chose this church…from all the rest…

WHO WAS ADAM'S MOTHER?

Who was Adam's mother?
How did God bring him to life?
God made him from dirt!
He did not need a wife
The Holy Spirit found the "Virgin Mary"
A woman pure and clean
Why do we doubt the virgin birth?
My God can do anything
How did God make the universe?
Where did he find the stones?
He merely spoke it into being
While sitting on His throne!
How did he make the moon and stars?
How did he make the sun to shine?
He's Omnipotent and everywhere you see
HE IS DIVINE!

BEYOND THE REACH OF GOD

Beyond the reach of God
A point where things become too hard
Another day of doubt and dismay
A way out of trouble there seems no way
Problems, worries, cares, and woes
Enemies, beggars, strangers, and foes
Why does there seem to be no end
Of things to fix, repair and mend
Put one thing together and another breaks
The more you try there are only more mistakes
Beyond the reach of God
But He's not beyond the reach of you
For problems there are answers,
for doubt there's faith
For sorrows there's joy, for hurt there's grace
Beyond the reach of God
May not seem so true
If only you can look into your heart
And know that He sees you
He knows what's really in your heart
And what He knows most of all
He's only just a prayer away.

He's just right down the hall
He's only just outside the door
Waiting for your call
There's no problem too big for Him
And there's none that is too small.

The Second Creation

Adam said I'm lonely
I'll ask God for a woman
God put him asleep on the ground
And walked upon the sand
God made a woman named Eve
And then he gave her to man
He made her soft and beautiful
He made her compassionate
He made her good to look at
That man could not forget
He gave her eyes
He gave her lips
He gave her a beautiful form
He made her soft and tender
Gave her arms to keep him warm
Now when Adam wakes each day
He thanks his God above
For the magnificent partner by his side
Sent by God to give him love.

Angels Then and Now

In revelations there were seven angels
to the seven churches given by God with love
I think they have been re-incarnated
into the Dolton Book Club.
Angels are special creations
and of that you can have no doubt
Powerful, divine, and heavenly
and of whom the world cannot do without
We have Michael, Gabriel
and Mary the mother of God
What would this world be like
with no one to encourage your heart
Sometimes you feel like crying
and don't know the reason why
Just know your personal angel
is always standing by
Thelma, Rhonda, Annette, Ann, Mary, Pat
and Pat add, Judy, Barbara and Rakiye
and you can't get much better than that.

No Prayer, No Power, No Love

Little prayer
little power
little Love

More prayer
more power
more Love

Lot of prayer
lot of power
Lot of love
Let love reign from the heightening Allegheny's
of Pennsylvania,
Let love reign from the curvaceous slopes
of the Rocky Mountains in California,
Let Love reign from
Lookout Mountain in Tennessee
Let Love reign from Stone Mountain in Georgia
Then we'll all be able to speed up
that bright day when we can say,

LOVE AT LAST….LOVE AT LAST…
THANK GOD ALMIGHTY
LOVE AT LAST!

SECTION II
SOCIOLOGICAL POEMS

Ernest R. Wallace

WHEN ROSES LAST IN THE DOORYARD BLOOMED

Lilacs last bloom in our dooryard[1.]
when Lincoln died
When John, Martin, and Robert died
The world prayed, fell on their knees and cried
John said, "What can you do for your country?"
Martin Said, "How long will the violence go on?"
Bobby picked up the banner
and then one day he was gone
How long? Not long. How long? Not long.
When will America again be strong?
A rose begins and lives from a tiny seed
A nation dies when too many of it's leaders bleed
Can Lilacs and Roses bloom again?
Can this dark world recover from all the pain?

[1.] A paraphrase taken from Walt Whitman's poem,
"When Lilacs Last In The Dooryard Bloomed."

WHEN YOU FAIL

When you fail all is not lost
Take inventory and count the cost
Evaluate what you've learned
Strike a match and start a burn
Create a flame of all you've failed
Launch a ship or raise a sail
Dig a hole or fill one up
Empty a pitcher or fill a cup
Don't let losses keep you down
Lift your head and look around
See the things yet undone
New horizons have begun
When you think you've reached your end
Start all over, just begin.

WHAT I DON'T KNOW

Do you know how to make a rocket ship?
Do you know how to make a train?
Do you know how to make a tall oak tree?
Do you know how to make a brain?
Questions I should ask myself
Questions you should ask too
When considering all the things in this world
Most of them are all brand new
Do I know how to make a sky?
Do I know how to make rain?
Socrates two thousand years ago
Said he didn't know anything
The more I read the more it shows
I'm not close to wisdom
But have a long way to go
I might as well relax
And in life begin to learn
For on every road and journey
There are new things at every turn!

Weak as Chinese Tea

Weak as Chinese Tea
What black leadership appears to be
A lot of volume
But not much substance
The flavor is there
But so is the pretense
A façade of power
But the void is immense
Top water, top water, top water
Weak as Chinese Tea
There is no real black leadership
For of the iceberg we only see the tip
Top water speeches, sermons and all
There is no depth, no power and no call
To be ordained by God you must be sent
Many were called but others only went!

Ode to the Pharaoh with no Nose

The Great Pyramid in Egypt
has a sphinx with no nose
It was blown off by Napoleon
so history would not propose
That a leader of this great nation
was a man with dark skin
The king of the people and all of their kin
This sphinx stands today as part of the great land
Defaced of all glory, it rests in the sand
What caused the Corsican to panic and so
Had the nose blown off by a cannon below?
He was the Emperor of the nation of France
Why was he afraid
to let a black man have a chance
A chance to be known by history as great
A ruler of nations, the supreme head of state
He had his kingdoms,
Bonaparte's on many thrones
Why couldn't' he just leave the
Great Sphinx alone?
There are many statues in Egypt today
That also had their noses blown away.

A Letter to Socrates

Petraca wrote a letter to Cicero
I wrote a letter for Socrates to know
Oh great teacher I'm writing to say
That what you've created, is alive today
The methods you founded on inquiry
That was taught in the schools of antiquity
To push for further reasoning and find
A greater answer or a greater mind
Perhaps with inquiry nothing has changed
But the truth is now closer
Despite lack of gain
Your "Socratic" method was
taught so men would know
To challenge the philosophies of the status quo
Men's search for honesty and Truth will be blessed
At the end of inquiry and their mind is at rest
Knowing that the "Truth is the Truth."
When they could have given up
and said…what's the use!

Ernest R. Wallace

THE NEGRO QUESTION?

What…is America to you?
Last hired, first fired, no revenue
Poll tax, Jim Crow
A living hell here on earth below
No flag, no country, no place really to go
Low esteem, white folks are mean,
what do you have to show
The white man says, a name, a flag, a place I see
A certain word democracy.
Democracy for him, but not for you
For America is an oligarchy
and that's really true…
You can't live in his neighborhood
For with you like the Jew your money is no good.
You can drive a Cadillac, a Benz,
or even a Rolls Royce
But like a fish out of water where you can live
You don't have much choice
What is America to you?
Neglected, rejected even with revenue
You can sing in his night clubs
and install his telephone

Try to buy a house next to his
and find that you are not in the zone
What…What …What…Is America to you?
Over there, over there,
we won't be back till it's over—over there
Well you went over there
You got shot over there
You survived and came back over here
And when you got home,
where the buffalo roams
And the deer and the antelope play
You were just as black
When you got back
"And the sky is not cloudy all day"
What…What…What is America to you?

Ernest R. Wallace

I cannot Change my Name To pawlikowski

I was born an American citizen
of parents who were both born free
I received a good elementary education
from James B. Ward School you see

I was graduated number one in my class
but as I grew older
I found that America cannot forget its past
I started high school at Tilden Technical,
a pre-engineering school

The best secondary education in Chicago
at that time that you could get
As a rule I transferred to John Marshall
known as the Commandos

The greatest school in Illinois,
as far as athletics goes
I was graduated from Marshall in 1963
in the top ten of my class,

But it was onto the City Colleges for me
I was athletic, academic

and finished seventh in my class
But I still had the feeling that

America could not forget its past
I worked a job while I attended school
and I burned the midnight oil as many others
would do I persevered
and got an Associate of Arts Degree
again in the top of my class

Was graduated Magna Cum Laude
I brought my degree to my job at last and found
that America could not forget its past
They took my degree and filed it away
and did nothing with it until my retirement day

I cannot change my name to Pawlikowski
For I am a male, black,
an African American you see

I don't feel inferior
and the city college was not my last stop
I'm now at Northwestern University
and academically still at the top.

LOVE…AMERICAN STYLE

God is Love and Love is God
All of it happens in the heart
The more you give, the more you get
No one has used love up yet
It's good for you, it's good for me
It's good from "sea to shinning sea"
God blessed America,
now America must bless God
America must put God back, in it's heart
We "say" we're all equal, we "say" we're all free
"My country tis of thee, sweet land of liberty"
But… "Truth forever on the scaffold and wrong
Forever on the throne"
We need love in our streets but most of all…
we need love at home.

GOD IS NOT A REPUBLICAN

God is not a republican
He doesn't need a running mate
He's the only one on the ticket
And He's God in every state
His name is in every hall of justice
And printed on every American coin
You can't make an appointment to talk to him
Unless you've been Reborn
No one can nominate Him
Or impeach Him from His throne
But if you're in the Royal Family
You can call Him on the phone
For Central is never busy
He's always on the line
And in case you can't get in touch
He is a friend of mine
We talk of separation of churches
and of state
But God is over them all
He decides who is President
and who walks in the Vatican's halls!

Ernest R. Wallace

AN ODE TO GWENDOLYN BROOKS

Hello Gwendolyn, how are you today?
I only saw you once before you passed away

I saw you one night in a Borders Book Store
I sat and listened to your poetry
And as you read I longed for more

You read with verve, sympathy and grace
You read stories about black people,
my people, my race

You read about people and place I've known
You gave perspectives of how God feels
Looking down from His throne

Why did you leave us, God only knows
Perhaps you were tired of life's sorrows and woes

In your book you signed sincerely
and penned the words to 'hold on'

I'm glad I met you that night
for eight months later you were gone.

THE FLIGHT OF A DREAM

We have dreams, wishes, desires, and goals.
They soar to the heavens all strong and bold,
Strong like a lion and wise like a fox,
But life is elusive and full of paradox
Like a man in a boat on a vast lonely ocean
Dying of thirst with water everywhere
Drink from the ocean for he knows not to dare
To yield to temptation won't release his thirst
He must ponder and wait for what to do first
Some dare to dream…and some will not…
We pay for our dreams…"Believe it or Not."
We pay for our dreams
with blood, sweat, and tears
We pay with our
souls…our hearts…and our years…
Don't be afraid…dream if you must…
Chose your dream wisely, then give it your trust
Follow your dream like an eagle on high
Not like a buzzard waiting for something to die
If…you don't reach it don't live in dismay
Your dreams made you better
than you were yesterday.

Eaama, Eaama, to Thee I Sing!

EAAMA, EAAMA, TO THEE I SING!!
DIVERSITY TO YOU WE BRING!

The knowledge, wisdom, and gifts we possess
With God and time can be made manifest
A richer life we strive to have
A better life we're going to have

EAAMA, EAAMA, TO THEE I SING!!
To all the world we are answering
the call to service, growth and peace
To attain life's highest, not it's least
A richer life we strive to have
A better life we're going to have

EAAMA, EAAMA TO THEE I SING!!
A name well worth remembering
A name of honor, a name of pride
With courage enough to stem the tide
A richer life we strive to have
A better life we're going to have

EAAMA…EAAMA…EAAMA…

A Country that Loses its Love

A country that loses its' love
Has failed to look to God above
To honor and love your fellow man
Is the only thing God can understand?
To say, "God Bless America" and not love all of us
Is a sign America has forgotten His son Jesus
To talk to God you must go through His son
To talk to His son you must go through everyone
God said, "You pray to me
whom you have never seen,
But persecute my children
and treat them cruel and mean."
God's letting America know
if it wants to be blessed
Don't love only your chosen few
but love all the rest
We continue to say, "God Bless America."
And tragedies continue to come
The only way to hear from Heaven
Is to recognize His only begotten son
"Jesus, Jesus, Jesus,
there is something about that name
Kings and kingdoms shall all pass away…
But there is something about that name…"

REAL AMERICAN FREEDOM

One man's freedom is another man's obligation
Until we are all free we will never be a free nation

Freedom doesn't come
just from the "Constitution"
Freedom must be pervasive in our institutions

No one in our communities,
neighborhoods and homes

Should ever feel that they are left all alone
America's not just a location, town or place

America will be America
when it's imbued with God's Grace

"Not by power, not by might but by My Spirit."
God said, then freedom's right

We have the "Iron Curtain"
and the "Cotton Curtain."

But when the curtain in the "Temple" was rent
God gave His Spirit: by the Holy Ghost it was sent

Until the people of America
have the Spirit God sent to man

America won' have purple mountains majesty
But a fruitless plain and barren land.

A Man Called King

Martin Luther King went to school all of his life,
Endured the crucible of high education
   in order to resolve racial strife
Dr. King said, "A threat to peace anywhere is a
   threat to peace everywhere."
So he enrolled at Morehouse College
   to begin to prepare
Prepare for a life that he could not foresee
He went to the mountaintop for you...and for me...
At Morehouse he met a man
   who would change all his ways
He came under the leadership
   of Dr. Benjamin Mays
Dr. Mays a great man of wisdom and insight,
   saw in young Martin King
   the champion of American civil rights
He had a dream and he gave it his all,
   From the red hills of Georgia
   to the nations great halls
From Montgomery to Selma,
   to Chicago and back
He fought discrimination though under attack

In Mississippi and Birmingham
he took a great stand,
Got stabbed and shot for the rights of man,
The wheels of justice grind slow
but oh...so very fine
Dr. Martin Luther King was
God's gift to all of mankind!
"We as a people will get to the promise land."
If we keep '**The Dream**' alive
and then take our stand.

AMERICA: BLACK AND WHITE

America…Black and White
America…Day and night

We'll never bridge the gap between I and you
Move forward we refuse to do

Martin Buber said, "An IF… For an I…Thou"
America, America heal your prejudice somehow

Our hair is different; our color is not the same
We fragment 'the races' by things most inane

America…black and white
America…day and night.

SECTION III
POEMS OF SECULAR LOVE

Yours...Now, Henceforth and Forevermore

I married you once I'd marry you again
For twenty years we've been friends

Friends, lovers need to be
Lovers that are not friends would cease to be

Cease to be lovers to the end
God wants you united through thick and thin

When God sends a mate He intends it for life
That's why I asked you to be my wife

A three fold cord can't be broken in two
There's us and God who will see us through

He holds your hand and He holds mine
With our hands in God we will be just fine

We'll walk through the valley of the shadows side by side
With God in front, He'll be our guide

He'll lead us to His home on high
Where we'll live forever in the sweet bye and bye

I married you once
I'd marry you again
For thirty more years we'll be friends

Friends forever until He calls us home
To one day stand before His great throne

To live together for eternity
In the mansion He's prepared for you and me.

Ernest R. Wallace

The Special Touch

You see a brother standing on a corner
With really no place to go
Looking north and looking south
For what…who really knows?
He has this serious look
As if something is on his mind
It's really just a façade you see
For he has nothing but time
He has no place to go
and nothing to come back to
So he stands in one spot all day long
with nothing really to do
Just like the Statue in New York Harbor
he stands there every day
In his mind, he thinks he's traveling
but it's just a one-act play
no prologue, epilogue, antagonist and such
It's his play…his only play
but with his special touch.

PARTHENIA'S CHILDREN

Parthenia was a country girl
Born in Memphis, Tennessee
Diminutive in size
But had six children you see
She took her education as far as she could
All six of her children excelled
And that was very good
Master teachers, singers, architects and engineers
Vindicated her sufferings, sacrifices and tears
She pushed her children, loved them
And gave them all she had
All of her children rose to the top of their fields
And that's not very bad
Parthenia was not an icon
As many of her children came to be
Who could imagine that all from one family
Come athletes, coaches, musicians
and leaders of various degrees
She made our home a place of love
A place we wanted to be
Now she's safe in the hands of God for all eternity.

ODE TO A LOST LOVE

Can you by searching find out God?
It's more than difficult, it's more than hard,

Can you imagine just how I feel?
Can you believe it's love and it is real!

As real as the tears I shed now and then
When I think of you and what could have been

I never knew how to love in vain
Till I loved you, lost you, and felt the pain

The pain I've seen through the tears of time
The pain of knowing you'll never be mine

I told you I loved you and told you again
I'm sorry, it's my fault we can only be friends

Oh! How I love you…did you ever know
What joy you brought me? You thrilled my soul.

If ever you loved me I'll never know
But I'm not afraid this time to tell you so…

I Dream of Nancy

I dream of Nancy when she sings
She's so ethereal she must have wings
When I see her face it has this glow
She must be from Heaven to radiate so
With a voice so pure and melody so divine
Her songs touch my heart time after time
A heavenly creation as everyone know
No one else like you on earth below
When you sing a song and hit E-flat
That note belongs only to you
No other can make it sound like that!

    This poem was written about one of my favorite singers of all time. Everyone knows her as a very elegant lady, Nancy Wilson.
    I wrote this poem after hearing her perform at the Fairmont Hotel Auditorium one night.
    This poem is dedicated to Nancy Wilson.

OUR MAJESTIC ROYAL LOVE

I am a king in the life of my love
My love is a queen sent from heaven above
Our love is royal like a pageant in Rome
When we're locked in embrace
our hearts are at home
When I feel the softness and warmth
of your touch
My body can only say…nothing too much,
nothing too much
Royalty is a privilege only a few can know
Like your love for me that makes me
glow, glow, glow
Your love is the palace that covers my heart
You arms are the gates that open
and gives me a start
Your lips are the embers that make me red hot
The warm touch of your body
lets me know what I've got
As I plunge into the perfume and waters
of your love
I feel your warm essence
like the softness of a dove
Flowers blossom and roses bloom
But the fragrance of your embrace fills my room
A king and queen may sit on their throne
And when I'm wrapped in your arms
I know we have a world of our own!

THE MAGIC OF AUTUMN

Oh!...isn't it wonderful to look and see,
The kaleidoscope of colors from tree to tree
On a branch, a bus, or on the ground
The most magnificent colors
in the world to be found
Obviously the work from
the Architect from above
That has touched nature with His brush
and a finger of love
A rainbow of hues and a sight to behold
Autumn is seen every year but never grows old
Always beautiful but never quite the same
From the fruited mountains to a western plains
Heraclitus said,
"You can never step in the same river twice."
But it really doesn't matter for it's just as nice
The cool touch of the water, a brook as it flows
is a precious silvery sight
before the first winter snows
The water is pure and good to touch
Another evidence that God loves us so much
The tall trees on the mountaintops
and valleys so green
Another rainbow of colors where God can be seen
Yes, autumn is magic like the coming of dawn
Take time to look at it carefully
for it too will soon be gone!

THE LOVE OF MY LIFE

Oh how I love Jesus,
Oh how I love you
Jesus is wonderful
And you're wonderful too
Lilies of the Valley
Bright and morning star
Do you really know
How beautiful you are?
Solomon was King,
Arrayed in all his glory
I wish you were my queen,
That would be the end
To the very great story
Why do I love you
Love you so much
I guess it's the joy
And warmth of your touch
When I see you first enter a room
My heart beats violently
Can't you hear the boom
Your eyes sparkle and twinkle so
I know you love me
And I love you more.

I Must Go Down to The Sea

I must go down to the sea
I must go down to the sea
To walk along the sand and shore
And sit under the shade of a tree
To hear the wind and feel the breeze
That brings calm to my soul
and makes me feel at ease
I must go down to the sea
To view the waves flowing endlessly in
The cool touch of the air caressing my skin
Before me I embrace the sand and sea
As the presence of God washes over me
I must go down to the sea
On the shore visions of nature talk back to me
We're locked in dialogue pure and free
I hear the foot steps in the sand
I reach out to the wind and hold it's hand
I feel the touch of the bright morning sun
As I caress the promises of a new day begun
I must go down to the sea
And take in revelations it always gives me
What do the winds and waves have to say
Take heart, have joy, for we're here to stay
We were here at creation, we'll be here next year
We'll never leave you, of that have no fear.

Ernest R. Wallace

A Grecian Musical Ode

A piano in the wilderness besides a big oak tree
A piano in the wilderness
playing beautiful melodies
Leaves are falling from the trees
All orange, yellow, and red
Autumn is here of this much can be said
It's Indian Summer, the weather is warm
But where are the beautiful melodies
coming from the grass, the oak tree
and piano are there
And the piano bench is empty and bare
Where do the wonderful music
and sounds come from
For the piano is vacant in the warm autumn sun
The sounds are pleasant, choral and free
But no musician is there to touch a key
It's so mystical and ethereal in sound
The music like nature is all around
Beethoven, Mozart and Brahms are all gone
But where do these beautiful chords come from?

FIVE MINUTES TO TWO

Five minutes to two
My main doctor came through
His name is Ham Lee
And he knows about me
Five minutes to two
Dr. Defranco is there too
Sitting at his desk
Making sure I have the best
Five minutes to two
Two technicians I knew
For weeks I was daily in their care
A pain chart they had so I would not despair
Five minutes to two
The day's now half through
My wife and my preacher now stand by my side
Letting me know that God is my guide
Five minutes to two
My surgery's now due
A needle in my hand so the pain I can stand
Five minutes to two
The surgery's all through
A sign that it's almost time to go home
The nurse for today is John Ardizone.

THE FIRST SPRING THAW

The first spring thaw with the melting of snow
Is beautiful because of the harsh winter before
The water drops falling crystalline and bright
Are made possible because of winter's long night
When the green grass shows
where the white snow stood
It has a miraculous affect
on our attitude for good
The birds are now singing
the trees now have leaves
We pause and reflect in the midst
of a warm summer breeze
The snow can be pretty, luminous and bright
But something about spring
is precious in our sight
The seasons come and the seasons go
The falling of rain, freezing,
and blowing of snow
But something happens
with the transition called spring
Which makes people happy
and gives meaning to everything.

THE BABY NO ONE CAN HOLD

The baby's name is Cayla
As beautiful as can be
She has this little cherub face
That's sweet and heavenly
She has these little chubby arms
And the cutest little jaws
Only eight months old right now
Can't walk but only crawl
Eat she does and all the time
Any kind of food is fine
If you don't feed her and on time
She'll holler and scream
And let you know what's on her mind
Why is she the baby that no one can hold?
It's a simple phrase of two words
The story can be told
SHE'S HEAVY.

As I Lay Dying

As I lay dying
she stood there smiling

As I lay dying
she was beguiling

As I lay dying
she never shed a tear

As I lay dying,
she never showed any fear.

TO HAVE LOST AT LOVE THREE TIMES

There are three women in the world
Just right for a man
To win the heart of one is a master plan
One out of three is not too bad
But to lose all three is really sad
To love and be loved by the one you love
Is a special gift from God above
To love and never have it returned
Is like a soul in Hades waiting to burn
You love someone and love them strong
Nothing they do can ever be wrong
Except when they fail to love you as much
Except when they don't feel your tender touch
You love them but they don't love you
Love them you must what else can you do
Like a broken winged bird high in the sky
Your love takes off but it cannot fly
It has "the wind beneath its wings"
But when one is broken it cannot sing
Birds like love soon fly away
As the setting sun brings the end to the day
Maybe the sun will rise tomorrow
With hope of new love and the end of my sorrows.

MY BROTHER ARTHER W. WALLACE

My brother, our brother, a wonderful son
Farewell, farewell, but I'll never let you go
You were a gift to our family but how much
only God can know
You'll live on in our spirit
and in our hearts you will stay.
It's hard to conceive that you've been taken away
brother, brother, husband and son
Father and uncle, so special to every one
Arther, you were truly one of a kind
A better brother we could not find
Time has come and now has gone
Your family must get closer and carry on
Like the wind we know not from
where it comes
Arther is now marching
to the beat of a different drum
If we could change things and make you stay
We would hold on to you for another day
Where the wind comes from and where it goes
is a mystery to our mortal souls.
My brother, our brother, a wonderful son
Your life was a gift to every one!

A Poem dedicated to my brother Arther W. Wallace.

Authors Profile

Ernest R. Wallace

The first poem I ever wrote was when I was sixteen years old. I was a student at Marshall High School in Chicago. Our track team had just won a third-place finish in the Illinois State Meet.

This victory for our team motivated me to write my first poem.

Over the later years of my life, poems came to me but I was not interested in writing them down. I was overseas in the United States Air Force, and the poems started coming to me again, but I didn't care about poems or recording them. For many years, the poems continued to pop into my head but I just dismissed them.

As I got older, the poems were more compelling, than they were when I was younger. By that time, I wrote more, and I could not rest until I wrote them down. The majority of my poems came to me around 2 a.m. About twelve years ago, I began to write all my poems as they came to me. The poems in this book, Poems from the Heart, are those that I have been inspired to write over the past decade.

❖ ❖ ❖

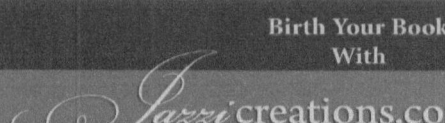

YOUR WEALTH IS MORE THAN JUST MONEY
LEAVE A LEGACY!

PUBLISH YOUR OWN BOOK

JAZZI CREATIONS SELF-PUBLISHING SERVICE, provides the professional assistance and preparation for book publishing

JAZZI CREATIONS, will guide you through a step by step self-publishing process and provide the resources necessary to bring your manuscript to a polished book that will make you proud.

JAZZI CREATIONS, is a unique company that produces transformational insight regarding those stories that you have dreamed about writing for years. Those stories are waiting for immediate release. Our main goal is to help bring the book that you have written to fruition.

By publishing your book through **JAZZI CREATIONS**, you are choosing an affordable and convenient way to achieve first-rate digital publication.

The Self Publishing process starts with your manuscript submission.

Even if you are not a writer we can ghostwrite your story. You will own and retain all rights to your project because we are here to provide a service. Once finished we turnover your book to you to sell and the profits remain yours.

**JAZZI CREATIONS
SELF-PUBLISHING SERVICE**
offers workshops
for youth and adults

Writing a book is not something that takes great talent—it takes great determination and will power.

For more information on this wonderful opportunity
Email:publisher@jazzi.com
Or
Visit our website:
www.jazzicreations.com

www.ingramcontent.com/pod-product-compliance
Lightning Source LLC
Chambersburg PA
CBHW020702300426

44112CB00007B/484